D0131458

Rookie
Read-About® Science

The Wheat
We Eat

By Allan Fowler

Consultants
Linda Cornwell, Learning Resource Consultant,
Indiana Department of Education

Jan Jenner, Ph.D.

New   ney
Danbury, Connecticut

Visit Children's Press® on the Internet at:
http://publishing.grolier.com

Designer: Herman Adler Design Group
Photo Researcher: Caroline Anderson

Library of Congress Cataloging-in-Publication Data

Fowler, Allan.
  The wheat we eat / by Allan Fowler.
    p. cm. – (Rookie read-about science)
  Includes index.
  Summary: Discusses the growing, processing, and eating of wheat, one of the
most common types of grain in the United States.
    ISBN 0-516-21212-5 (lib. bdg.)   0-516-26569-5 (pbk.)
    1. Wheat— Juvenile literature. [1. Wheat.] I. Titles. II. Series.
  SB191.W5F426   1999   98-25099
  641.3'311—dc21   CIP
                                                          AC

GROLIER
PUBLISHING

Rookie
Read-About® Science

The Wheat
We Eat

By Allan Fowler

Consultants
Linda Cornwell, Learning Resource Consultant,
Indiana Department of Education

Jan Jenner, Ph.D.

New   ney
Danbury, Connecticut

Visit Children's Press® on the Internet at:
http://publishing.grolier.com

Designer: Herman Adler Design Group
Photo Researcher: Caroline Anderson

Library of Congress Cataloging-in-Publication Data

Fowler, Allan.
    The wheat we eat / by Allan Fowler.
      p. cm. – (Rookie read-about science)
    Includes index.
    Summary: Discusses the growing, processing, and eating of wheat, one of the
most common types of grain in the United States.
    ISBN 0-516-21212-5 (lib. bdg.)   0-516-26569-5 (pbk.)
    1. Wheat—Juvenile literature. [1. Wheat.] I. Titles. II. Series.
SB191.W5F426   1999   98-25099
641.3'311—dc21   CIP
                                       AC

GROLIER
PUBLISHING
1 2 3 4 5 6 7 8 9 10 R 08 07 06 05 04 03 02 01 00 99

Have you eaten any wheat
today? Many breakfast cereals
are made from wheat.

Did you eat a sandwich for lunch? White bread and whole wheat bread are made from wheat.

Did you eat spaghetti
for dinner? Pasta is
made from wheat, too.

Wheat is a grassy plant.

Wheat is also the name of
the seeds that come from
a wheat plant.

The wheat plant belongs
to a family of plants
called cereals.

Corn, rice, oats, rye, and
barley are all cereal plants.

Most of the cereals we
eat for breakfast are made
from cereal plants.

Rye

Oats

Wheat

Barley

Seeds of cereal plants are called grains. Rye seeds, oat seeds, wheat seeds, and barley seeds are all grains.

Corn kernels are also
a type of grain.

More people in the world eat rice than any other type of grain.

But in North America, people eat more wheat than rice.

Most of the wheat we eat is grown in the Great Central Plains of Canada . . .

Drummond, New Brunswick, Canada

Jackson County, South Dakota

. . . and the United States.

Many farmers grow two
crops of wheat a year.

Spring wheat usually
has red grains.

It is planted in the
spring and harvested
in the summer.

Winter wheat usually has white grains. It is planted in the fall and harvested in the spring.

Winter wheat

At one time, farmers plowed fields with oxen and planted wheat seeds by hand.

When the plants were full grown, farmers had to reap the wheat (cut it down) . . .

. . . and thresh it (separate
the seeds from the straw)
by hand.

Today machines do most of the work.

One person can operate
a machine that reaps and
threshes a field of wheat.

After the grain is harvested,
it goes to a mill. In the past,
mills were powered by water.

At the mill, the outer coats—called husks—are removed from the seeds.

Have you ever eaten a bran muffin?

Wheat bran is made from wheat husks.

To make flour, the grain is ground and sifted many times.

There are many types of wheat. Pastas are made from wheat with the hardest grains.

Breads are made from wheat with hard grains. Cookies and cakes are made from wheat with soft grains.

To make bread dough, water and other ingredients are added to flour.

If yeast is added,
the dough will rise.

At one time, people baked
bread themselves. Today most
bread is made in factories.

Have you ever smelled baking bread? Wheat gives us many good things to eat—and smell.

Words You Know

wheat plant

wheat seeds

reap

thresh

dough

grains

pasta

31

Index

About the Author

Allan Fowler is a freelance writer with a background in advertising. Born in New York, he lives in Chicago now and enjoys traveling.

Photo Credits